North Staffordshir

Scenes From The 1980s

Terry Moors

Landmark Publishing

Published by

Ashbourne Hall, Cokayne Ave
Ashbourne, Derbyshire, DE6 1EJ England
Tel: (01335) 347349 Fax: (01335) 347303
e-mail: landmark@clara.net

1st Edition

13 ISBN: 978-1-84306-347-6

British Library Cataloguing in Publication Data: a catalogue record for this book is available from the
British Library.

Print: Cromwell Press
Design by: Michelle Hunt

Front Cover: Class 47, 47568 at Knutton, with a coal train from Holditch colliery, on 18 March 1987.
Back Cover Main: Permanent-Way gang at Kidsgrove Station, 20 April 1986.
Back cover Bottom Left: Longport Junction Signal Box, June 1986.
Page 3: Signalman and Shunter at Alsager East Signal Box, 25 November 1984.

North Staffordshire Railways
Scenes From The 1980s

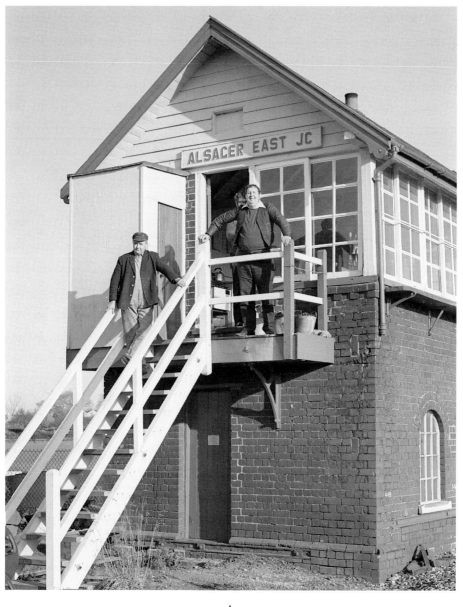

Landmark Publishing

CONTENTS

GLOSSARY

ECS	Empty Coaching/Carriage Stock
Diagram	A schedule designed to obtain the most efficient working arrangement for train crews, locomotives and rolling stock.
Head shunt	A length of track, which allows shunting movements to be made into a cluster of sidings without fouling the running lines to which it is connected.
LMS	London Midland & Scottish Railway
MGR	Merry-go-Round. A system of operating continuously moving permanently coupled trains between collieries and electricity generating power stations.
NSR	North Staffordshire Railway Company
TOPS	British Railways' computer-based Total Operations Processing System of freight wagon information, introduced in 1973. It details every event concerning freight traffic (and locomotives and other items of stock) and transmits this information over the whole of British Rail.
ZUV	Three-letter TOPS code (as an example) for a 'Shark' ballast plough. (codes for other types of freight wagons appear at various points in the text)

INTRODUCTION

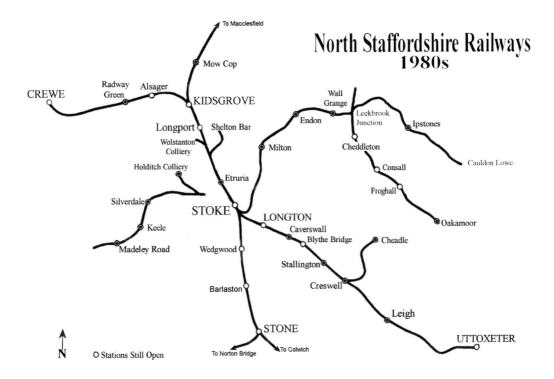

**North Staffordshire Railways
1980s**

To Macclesfield

Mow Cop

CREWE

Radway Green · Alsager · KIDSGROVE

Longport · Shelton Bar

Wolstanton Colliery

Holditch Colliery

Silverdale

Keele

Madeley Road

STOKE

Wedgwood

Barlaston

Etruria

Milton

Wall Grange

Endon · Leekbrook Junction · Ipstones

Cheddleton

Consall

Froghall

Cauldon Lowe

Oakamoor

LONGTON · Caverswall · Blythe Bridge · Cheadle

Stallington

Creswell

Leigh

STONE

To Norton Bridge · To Colwich

UTTOXETER

N · O Stations Still Open

I have heard it said that a railway enthusiast is an individual who supports a broad interest in railways, focused not by steam, diesel or electric traction alone but with the whole of the railway landscape. The reality however is not quite like that. There seems to be the steam enthusiast, who would not admit to recognising a diesel loco, and the modern traction enthusiast who would not admit knowing one 'kettle' from another! I was brought up in the age of steam and as a boy I was fascinated by the busy industrial steam engines, working out of Whitfield Colliery or shunting coal trains at Pinnox sidings in Tunstall, or the sight and sound of a Britannia rushing through Chatterley Valley working a Manchester-Euston express. It would seem therefore that I could easily fall into the category of committed steam enthusiast? Not a bit of it, I regard myself as a devoted railway enthusiast – enjoying all its diversity.

With the introduction of diesel locomotives and AC electrics during the late 1950s I had already acquired, much to the disbelief of some of my associates, an interest in these "growl boxes" and "hair dryers" – as so described by one of my steam-for-ever friends. Living at the northern boundary of Stoke-on-Trent at Goldenhill, my favourite "spotting" locations then were Kidsgrove and Crewe stations. It was at Kidsgrove, during the early sixties, that I became aware of the significant changes that were to remove steam altogether from British Railways and take out 5000 miles of the railway network. Although at that time I had the means at my disposal to photograph this changing scene, I omitted to do so. An oversight I regret to this day.

Tolerant of this oversight, my interest in railways never diminished and by 1980 I learned of plans by British Rail to transform yet again the areas' railway and its infrastructure. This time I was determined not to let another period of 'modernisation' pass without documenting at least some of it in photographs. And so, during the following ten years, I set about photographing locomotives and their trains, at the line-side, sidings, stations, signal boxes, branch lines, collieries surface railways and the dedicated railway staff who seemed so committed to their railway. Most of the photography covers North Staffordshire and therefore a large number of the pictures show scenes of a railway created originally by the North Staffordshire Railway Company, a great deal of which has now vanished altogether.

Kidsgrove, because of its junction status and being close to my home, was a favourite location through the 1980s. It was a busy junction with a wide variety of motive power to be seen. It was a hive of activity at week ends as regular permanent way work on the West Coast Main Line required trains to be diverted via Stoke and then 'dragged' by diesel power over the non-electrified branch between Kidsgrove and Crewe. I make no apologies for including a number of images of Kidsgrove at various points in the book but I hope that there is some merit in this by illustrating the many and varied

Silverdale Coal Loader with 20s, 20007 and 20047, 28 May 1986.

railway activities on this part of the line.

My job at the PMT during this time held certain advantages that enabled me to take a weekday off quite regularly, which gave me the opportunity to photograph some unusual train workings. The station staff at Kidsgrove became aware of my regular visits and over the years they were extremely helpful and informative. I made some good friends on the railway, in particular Harold Brough and Arthur Morris, both Leading Railman at Kidsgrove Station, and signalmen Eddie Hamilton and Ken Faulkner who worked at Milton Junction and Leekbrook Junction signal boxes. I take this opportunity to thank them all for their kindness, and through them, I extend my grateful thanks to all the other railway staff who spared their time to help me on so many occasions.

Also during my many visits to Kidsgrove during the 1980s I met a number of young 'trainiacs' who were so knowledgeable about modern railway operations and the information they gave me was so valuable, allowing me to be there at the right time to photograph a particular train. Their enthusiasm and friendship, without doubt, enabled me to capture a number of pictures that are included in this book. Consequently, my grateful thanks go to Jackie Barfoot, Peter Rawlins and Martin Steventon.

A few pictures in the book involve straying a little out of the decade in order to illustrate a particular place or activity that has now disappeared for good. An example is the set of pictures of steam workings at Chatterley Whitfield Mining Museum in 1992. I believe that given the current commercial situation at Whitfield, it is unlikely that a steam railway would ever return there.

I have taken care to ensure dates, times and locations are correct and I take full responsibility for any errors or omissions, which may be subsequently identified and I apologise for this. However, if any errors do appear, I would be grateful for the reader to advise me accordingly.

1. KIDSGROVE – CREWE

The North Staffordshire Railway Company opened the line between Kidsgrove (Harecastle) and Crewe on 9 October 1848. Interestingly, the line and its stations, located at Alsager and Radway Green (& Barthomley) survived largely unchanged until Radway Green closed to passengers on 7 November 1966. The next major change came as a consequence of the Crewe remodelling work when, in June 1985, the signal boxes at Alsager East Junction, Alsager Station and Radway Green were removed together with all block signalling on the line. This system was replaced with Multiple Aspect Signalling (MAS) controlled from the Crewe Control Centre. At the same time, the section of line between Radway Green and North Stafford Junction at Crewe was reduced to single line working.

When the West Coast Main-Line Upgrading reached this area in 2003 the line was completely re-laid and 25kv overhead catenary installed to provide an all-electric alternative route between Colwich Junction and Crewe.

On Sunday 20 June 1982, engineering work closed the main line between Kidsgrove and Macclesfield requiring trains to be diverted over the non-electrified line, via Alsager and Radway Green, to Crewe. At Kidsgrove Central on that day 25058 waits in platform 1 with a ballast train, while Class 40, 40155 comes off the Crewe branch with a diverted Manchester-Birmingham service.

Diesel Electric Multiple Unit (DEMU) prototypes 210-001 and 210-002 pass through Kidsgrove Central on Friday 10 September 1982 en route to Carlisle Upperby for a weekend appearance there. The duo returned to their base at Derby on Monday 13 September.

The driver of English Electric type 4, 40091 draws his train away from platform 3 at Kidsgrove Central with the return working of a summer Saturdays' Stoke-North Wales excursion. The date is 19 June 1982 and the number of passengers alighted from the train suggests that it was well patronised.

On 14 October 1989, standing in for the usual class 150 Sprinter units, class 37, 37431 with four Mk 2 coaches, slows for its scheduled stop at Kidsgrove Central whilst working the 1139 Crewe-Derby.

During the mid-1980s the Stoke area was blessed with a number of interesting enthusiast specials. One of the star attractions at that time was the National Collection's Type 4 40122 (D200) and it is seen here with "The Midland Executive" railtour leaving Kidsgrove Central on 2 June 1984, heading towards Crewe.

On a very cold 13 January 1985, class 101 two-car DMU works an unidentified Derby - Crewe service through Red Bull. Kidsgrove Central's Up Distant signal is in the foreground and the bridge behind the DMU carries the A34 road between Butt Lane and Congleton.

Looking South towards Kidsgrove on 4 December 1982 the signal is off for unidentified class 47 to enter the sidings at Alsager East Junction with its train of engineers spoil.

Looking North towards Alsager Station the same class 47, having run around its train, leaves Alsager East Junction for Stoke. The structures behind the signal box form part of the extensive Twyfords Sanitary Ware factory. 4 December 1982.

When this picture was taken on 25 November 1984, Alsager East Junction Signal Box had only 6 months operational life remaining before its demolition, in June 1985, as part of the Crewe remodelling work.

Inside the immaculately kept Alsager East Signal Box, the signalman sets the road for a Crewe–Derby service on 25 November 1984. The track diagram shows the extensive sidings, which were under the control of this signal box, with its Mackenzie & Holland 44 lever frame.

Four of the sidings at Alsager East Junction, located on the Up side were still in use when this picture was taken on 29 May 1985. Most of the wagons in this view are ZHVs used to convey ballast. The skyline is dominated by the Twyfords Sanitary Ware factory.

On 13 March 1985, class 120 3-car DMU passes Alsager East Junction with the 1420 Crewe-Lincoln.

Class 25, 25059 spent most of the day on 13 March 1985 working a permanent way train recovering track panels which were being removed from the west sidings. This was being done before the Crewe remodelling work, which would see this part of the railway completely transformed. Behind the train is the site of the former wagon repairers, Settle Speakman, which is being cleared and landscaped.

On 13 March 1985, 25059 departs in the afternoon from Alsager East Down sidings with track panels which were lifted earlier. Above and to the right of the train can be seen the derelict industrial land being cleared.

In a matter of only two months, further track work was removed and the area, once occupied by railway-related industry, is now transformed into open parkland. Passing the site on 29 May 1985, are English Electric type 2s 20182 and 20159 with the Oakamoor-St Helens sand train.

A variety of motive power appeared on a regular empty coaching stock (ECS) diagram to Derby. On 29 May 1985, 45062 was the locomotive of choice and the ensemble is seen heading, at speed, through Alsager Station.

Rare class 154 Sprinter unit, 154002, briefly visits Alsager Station on 20 August 1988, standing in for the more ubiquitous class 150 sets, whilst working the 1248 Derby-Crewe service.

On 26 June 1984, 47612 and 87010 head the 1150 Euston-Manchester through Alsager station en-route to Crewe. This was one of many diverted trains that summer due to regular weekend permanent way work between Kidsgrove and Macclesfield.

Unidentified class 47, with the diverted 1525 Manchester-Birmingham, powers through Alsager Station on a warm sunny Sunday in July 1984.

HST set 43178 rushes through Alsager Station on 26 June 1984 with the diverted 1050 Paignton-Manchester.

Another sunny Sunday in July 1984 and 25200 and an unidentified classmate amble through Alsager station with an empty ballast train, following weekend engineering work in the Kidsgrove area.

The North Stafford Railway company architecture of the signal box and station house at Alsager is evident in this view taken on 25 November 1984.

On the same day, I was invited by the signalman to photograph the inside of the signal box. The interior, as expected, was spotlessly clean and tidy so typical of these railway men and their commitment to the job. However this scene was, in a matter of months, to disappear forever when the box was demolished as part of the Crewe remodelling work.

Another view of Alsager Station signal box and crossing, this time on 12 March 1985. Note that this signal box was unique in being one of only two North Stafford Railway (NSR) signal boxes to have being built with a bay window. In Alsager's case, this allowed the signalman an unrestricted view of the road, which bends sharply at this point, before closing the gates.

When this picture was taken on 5 June 1985, the signal box had gone and Multiple Aspect Signalling (MAS) equipment was in use, with CCTV cameras covering the crossing. All of this was now managed entirely by the newly built Crewe Control Centre. The Up platform station buildings are an indication of the high status that Alsager Station once held. Sadly all this has now gone, to be replaced by a brick 'bus shelter'.

Passing the remains of Radway Green Station on 5 August 1984, 40155 is in charge of a BR Staff club "Stoke to Blaenau Ffestiniog" excursion.

Radway Green signal box on a fine summers day 26 July 1984. This was a typical NSR 'signal cabin' with a Mackenzie & Holland 20 lever frame.

The interior of Radway Green signal box on 2 December 1984. During World War 2, this box would have been extremely busy with ammunition train movements from the nearby Royal Ordnance Factory.

The signal box now but a memory, Intercity 125 set 253030 makes its way through unusual territory as it passes Radway Green Crossing while working the diverted Exeter St David's–Manchester service on 21 September 1986.

It is always a problem finding a satisfactory pathway for slow moving locomotives and this was the case on 14 August 1985, just North of Radway Green, when 08 Shunters 08450 (leading) and 08699 were on the move to Crewe Diesel Depot. 08699 was assigned shunting duties at Longport Yard but was subsequently damaged due to a derailment there. 08450 came to the rescue and the duo are seen here, about to enter the single line section which commences just beyond the M6 Motorway Bridge, visible in the distance.

On 24 March 1984, class 50 locomotive 50007 "Sir Edward Elgar" shatters the silence at Oakhanger as it thunders towards Crewe whilst working "The Border City" railtour. This section is now single line.

The first of three 'then and now' pages shows Cravens (class 120) DMU set 512 passing the crossing at Valley Brook with an afternoon Derby-Crewe service in July 1982. The crossing protects the railway from vehicles using the unclassified road between the villages of Oakhanger and Smith's Green.

Twenty one years later the same location witnesses Alphaline's class 158 DMU 158818 passing the crossing at Valley Brook with an unidentified service. The date is 12 October 2003, only days after the line was re-opened following months of work to replace all the track and installation of 25kv overhead line equipment, as part of the West Coast Main-Line Upgrade.

Just after leaving Crewe, North Stafford Junction, 47032 heads South past Bridgehouse Farm, with an engineers train, on 18 April 1985-still double track at this time.

It was a different scene on 6 July 2003 as General Motors (Ontario) class 66, 66057 moves slowly over newly ballasted rail during the West Coast Main-Line Upgrade. This is part of the single line section between Radway Green and Crewe and the columns to the right of the train are supports for the new overhead line equipment.

Heading north past Bridgehouse Farm, 25176 and 25224 power the Oakamoor-St Helens (Pilkington's Glass Works) sand train on the up - gradient towards Crewe on 18 April 1985.

The same location on 12 October 2003 witnesses a Virgin HST working an unidentified service diverted from the West Coast Main Line, along brand new track und under fully energised 25kv overhead lines.

2. UTTOXETER – CHEADLE – STOKE

The Stoke-Uttoxeter section of the North Staffordshire Railway Company's system opened on 7 August 1848. However, the 3.5-mile branch line from Cresswell Junction to Cheadle was not fully opened until 1901, taking 9 years to complete. Although the Cheadle branch line remained open for sand traffic until 1988, its timetabled passenger services ceased altogether on 17 June 1963. However, Cheadle Station witnessed passengers again for one day only in March 1985 when a charter train travelled the line to launch British Rail's Charter Train Unit. Three years on and the station had been demolished. During the following years, the sidings, together with a quarter mile section of track, were removed to make way for a new housing development and the signal boxes at Cresswell and Stallington were closed and demolished. This chapter gives a brief view of the Uttoxeter-Stoke line and the Cheadle branch before these changes took place.

Uttoxeter Station on 1 July 1984 with class 120 3-car DMU just arriving with the 1738 Lincoln-Crewe. The station at this time was a fragment of the original 4-platform junction with lines serving Derby, Ashbourne, Stoke and the Churnet Valley. During 2005 however, the station had a makeover funded by Staffordshire County Council and Central Trains to improve the passenger facilities, car parking and provision of a bus interchange.

Leigh Signal Box was the last of the North Staffordshire Railway Company's cabins, with wheel-operated crossing gates, closing on 11 July 1999. This view, taken on 22 June 1986, shows the original crossing gates, together with the oil burning lamps attached to each gate. This particular box was to have been re-located to Consall for use on the Churnet Valley Railway. Unfortunately, the roads around Leigh proved to be too narrow for it to be moved from the village and it was subsequently demolished.

On a warm July evening in 1982, class 120 DMU passes Cresswell sidings with a Lincoln-Crewe service. The buildings to the right of the train are part of the extensive Johnson Mathey Company, which manufactures colours for the nearby pottery industry. The sidings on the left were still in use at this time and the start of the Cheadle branch is just discernible behind the bracket signal.

This is a view of Cresswell Signal Box, photographed on 1 July 1984. The sidings here were still connected to the Cheadle branch for occasional use by sand trains. On this particular day though a rake of Presflo 'Tunnel' hoppers were marshalled and are seen opposite the signal box. Less than a year later, the Cheadle line would carry the first (and last) passenger train to Cheadle Station since it closed to passenger traffic in 1963.

Another view of Cresswell Signal Box looking towards Stallington from the area formerly occupied by the station and goods sidings. The impressive telegraph mast in the background was, by this time, devoid of any connecting wires. The signal box was closed in 1989 and replaced with automatic barrier operation. Photographed on 22 June 1986.

On 28 March 1985, a special with a difference – 47/4, 47532 of Crewe Diesel Depot, had charge of a selection of carriages, which included Pullman Rail's cars 353, 347 and 129, displaying to potential hirers the type of vehicle available from British Rail Inter City Sector, as they launched their Charter Train Unit. The train is seen here between Tean and Cheadle, on the branch that connects with the Stoke-Derby line at Cresswell Junction.

47532 arrives at Cheadle Station with its very special train of passengers who were to change here for road transport, namely coaches hired from the Potteries - based PMT bus company, for the short journey to the Alton Towers theme park. At this time the park was being developed by its owner John Broom who considered that bringing in visitors by rail could reduce road traffic to the Towers. The idea never proceeded beyond this day and, by 2007, the area around Alton continues to be blighted by seasonal traffic.

A great deal of interest was shown from local people as they gather on Cheadle Station's single platform to take pleasure in the unusual appearance of a passenger train there on 28 March 1985.

Even though 22 years had passed since passenger services were withdrawn from Cheadle, the station was in remarkably good condition when this picture was taken on 28 March 1985. The station never had the benefit of more than five passenger trains per day during its lifetime and it was extremely unlikely to have seen Pullman cars. Seen here though is Car No 353 being admired by a local resident.

The sight of a passenger train at Cheadle Station on 28 March 1985 was enough to bring local residents to investigate what was happening. In this photograph groups of children from nearby Cheadle High and Painsley RC Schools, under the supervision of teachers, check out 47532 after it had run around the train for its return working. In 1994, this area was cleared to make way for a new housing development, leaving just the station house, which is visible in the background.

The Stoke-Derby line produced a variety of motive power and on 3 July 1987 class 20s 20097 and 20042 made an appearance, seen here leaving Cresswell Junction with a ballast train bound for Cockshute Sidings.

By the mid 1980s, class 150 'Sprinters' had replaced most of the Cravens class 120 DMUs on the Crewe-Derby services. Seen here on 3 July 1987, between Stallington and Cresswell, is 150114 with the 1520 Crewe-Skegness.

LMS '8F' No 48151, newly restored when this picture was taken on 3 July 1987, rushes through Creswell with its support coach en route to the Crewe Heritage Centre opening weekend. Although under its own steam, the locomotive was required to be piloted from Caverswall to Crewe by class 47, 47439. During this period, British Rail banned the operation of steam locomotives under 25Kv overhead lines.

On 30 August 1986, 'Sprinter' 150109 approaches Stallington Crossing whilst working a late afternoon Derby-Crewe service. By this date, most of the class 120 DMU diagrams had all but disappeared.

Stallington Signal box, with its 13-lever McKenzie & Holland frame, came into use on 28 October 1884 and was built to the North Staffordshire Railway Company's own specification. The ornate bargeboards are one of the features copied by the NSR from signal boxes built by the Great Northern Railway. The brick base and arched locking-room windows however are typical McKenzie & Holland. This view, photographed on 30 August 1986, illustrates the wheel operated crossing gates and the level crossing keeper's house. The level crossing in fact existed some years before the signal box was established there

Another view of Stallington Signal Box, showing the pedestrian turnstile or 'Kissing Gate'. The turnstile was actually locked by the signalman as soon as the main crossing gates were closed to prevent anyone attempting to cross the line ahead of an oncoming train. The box was built to control crossover points, which allowed run-around movements at Blythe Bridge. Stallington signal box closed in 1989.

One of the shortest block sections on the North Staffordshire Railway lay between Blythe Bridge and Stallington. On 30 August 1986 class 150 'Sprinter' unit, 150147, is seen with an afternoon Crewe-Derby service. Blythe Bridge Station is just visible in the distance.

By the time this picture was taken on 28 April 1991, Blythe Bridge Station was condemned for demolition. Despite a great deal of local opposition to its removal, the station buildings were finally raised to the ground a few weeks later.

Caverswall Signal Box opened in 1942 when newly constructed goods loops were introduced here in order to handle increased wartime traffic. This particular box was built to a standard LMS design with an REC type lever frame. Unlike North Stafford boxes, Caverswall was quite plain with no ornate bargeboards and no windows provided to the locking-room.

From Caverswall the line descends towards Longton through Meir Tunnel, through which the 1630 Lincoln-Crewe DMU has just passed. When this picture was taken on 1 July 1984, class 120 DMUs were in sole charge of these services.

For the railway enthusiast who has a particular interest in signal boxes, Foley Crossing, situated just South of Longton Station, is easily overlooked since the very narrow Foley Road, on which the crossing stands, is not fully open to vehicular traffic. The box, which was built to the North Staffordshire Railway Company's own design with a McKenzie & Holland lever frame, is still in use. Photographed on 18 August 1985.

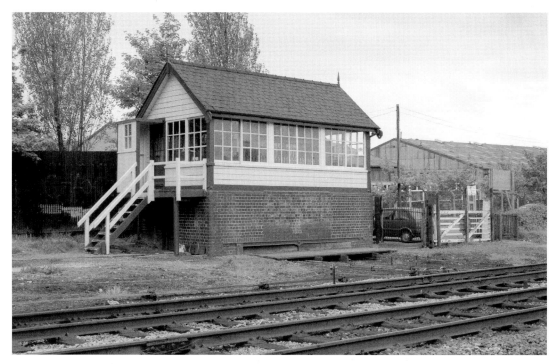

Another view of Foley Signal Box, taken on the same day, illustrates the standard practice of positioning entrance steps to face oncoming trains. When originally built in 1889 the brick base would have had two, arched locking-room windows to the front elevation. These have subsequently been bricked up but the outlines are just discernible.

On 16 May 1987, class 150 'Sprinter' 150123 approaches Longton with an afternoon Crewe-Skegness service. By this date the skyline had changed with no evidence of the once numerous bottle ovens and chimneys associated with the substantial pottery industry, which once dominated this area.

On the downhill stretch from Longton to Stoke Junction heavyweight 58002, with a Toton–Garston MGR, passes Smith's Pool, Fenton on 18 September 1986. The high ground in the distance is what remains of the former Glebe Colliery spoil tip, which was reclaimed and developed by the City Council as Glebedale Park.

On 18 June 1986, class 150 'Sprinter' 150123, having just left Stoke Junction, begins the long climb to Longton with the 1320 Crewe–Derby.

Another example of the varied motive power to be seen on this line is class 31, 31161 with a Crewe-Derby Empty Coaching Stock diagram, about to pass beneath Smithpool Road Bridge, Fenton, on 18 June 1986.

Leaving Stoke Junction on 1st March 1983, a class 120 DMU heads south on to the Derby line with an afternoon Crewe-Nottingham service. Behind the DMU, the electrified line to Stone, Norton Bridge and the Trent Valley is visible. In the foreground and to the left of the picture are the tracks to Pratts Sidings and the branch to Milton and Leekbrook Junction.

Entering platform 2 at Stoke Station is a class 120 DMU with the 1330 Derby–Crewe on 21 April 1982. The buildings to the right of the leading car form part of Stoke Goods Shed, part of which remains but in non-railway commercial use.

A busy scene at Stoke Station on 5 July 1984 as 25059 draws into platform 1 from Cockshute Sidings for a crew change. A poster on the far wall of platform 2 advertises a well-known food 'delicacy' associated with Stoke-on-Trent.

3. STOKE – LEEKBROOK – OAKAMOOR

The line to Leekbrook, originally opened in 1849 as the Biddulph Valley Line, begins at Stoke Junction, just south of the Station, running immediately under the A5007 City Road and past the former Pratts Sidings and heads east towards Bucknall, Milton, Endon and eventually Leekbrook Junction. At this point the lines from Oakamoor, Cauldon Lowe and the sidings that are now what remains of the line to Leek and North Rode, converge to form the Junction. Although sand traffic from Oakamoor ceased on 30 August 1988 and the contract for railway ballast terminated with Cauldon Lowe quarry in 1989, the lines remained. Because the lines were mothballed by BR, the North Staffordshire Railway Company (1978) Ltd and the Churnet Valley Railway (1992) plc were able to purchase the line between Leekbrook and Oakamoor Sand Sidings in 1995 and are now successfully operating trains from Cheddleton, Leekbrook and Froghall. This chapter illustrates the railway and its people in happier times, during the mid-1980s period when closure seemed possible but not inevitable.

On a very cold and wet morning of 6 April 1982, class 25s, 25042 and 25157 wait for the signal to depart Stoke Station with a train of 'empties' to Oakamoor sand quarry. Its journey involves two single line operations, first to Milton Junction where the staff is changed for a single line token for the second section to Leekbrook Junction.

The double track at Pratts Sidings appears well groomed on 1 March 1983 as 25262 slows for Stoke Junction with an Oakamoor-St Helens sand train. At this time, the line is still double track all the way to Milton Junction.

Just beyond Pratts Sidings, now taken over by vegetation, is the site of Fenton Manor Station, which closed to passengers on 7 May 1956. Passing this location, at the end of June 1986, two unidentified class 20s head for Stoke Junction with the afternoon Oakamoor-St Helens sand train. (Peter Rawlins)

Class 20s 20197 and 20165, in charge of the Oakamoor-St Helens sand train, seem to be working wrong line as they amble through Bucknall, towards Stoke, on 18 June 1986. By this date, single line working was in operation between Stoke and Milton Junction. What appears to be newly ballasted track is in fact a coating of sand, blown from passing trains.

The first of two level crossings on this line is met at Birches Head Road and is known as Abbey Crossing. When this picture was taken on 15 September 1985 the crossing keepers house was already in private ownership and the Milton Junction signalman, Eddie Hamilton, is closing the manually operated gates.

The operation of Abbey Crossing and associated signals are interlocked with Milton Junction signal box. Signalman Eddie Hamilton is seen here releasing the signal from Abbey Crossing Ground Frame on 15 September 1985.

On 15 September 1985, class 20s 20166 and 20183, in charge of the afternoon Oakamoor-St Helens sand train, are given the road to proceed through Abbey Crossing for the 3 mile run down to Stoke Junction.

Milton Junction signal box was, by 1867, controlling movement of trains on the lines from the Biddulph Valley, Leek and Stoke, all of which converged at this point. This view, looking northwest, was taken in May 1987 and shows the line from Leekbrook Junction in the foreground.

Another view of Milton Junction signal box this time taken from the track-bed of the former Biddulph Valley line, which was closed entirely in 1977 following the closure of Norton Colliery.

Inside Milton Junction signal box on 25 September 1985, signalman Eddie Hamilton operates the block instrument to accept a train from Stoke. Shown clearly is the McKenzie & Holland 34 lever frame and the single line apparatus situated behind the armchair.

In this view, taken on 13 May 1987, the Milton Junction signalman exchanges with the driver of 20060, the single line staff (from Stoke) for the single line token to Leekbrook Junction.

Although not strictly a junction at this time Milton Junction was the intermediate point for the two single line sections between Leekbrook and Stoke. Trains from Stoke were worked by a single line staff 'Stoke-Milton Jct' as shown here by the signalman at Milton Junction. The Milton to Leekbrook section was operated by tokens, released from the token apparatus interlocked to each signal box. (See page 53)

On 25 September 1985, Milton Junction signalman Eddie Hamilton exchanges the Leekbrook-Milton Junction token, for the single line staff to Stoke, with the second man of 20166 and 20183 which were in charge of the Oakamoor-St Helens sand train.

An earlier view of Milton Junction, taken in 1983, and the signal box complete with its original name board. Also in the picture are class 25s, 25161 and 25197 with the afternoon Oakamoor-St Helens sand train.

On 19 June 1980, the North Staffordshire Railway Company (1978) Ltd arranged for the first passenger train to Cheddleton Station since closure in 1965. These DMU specials, known as the 'Churnetrail' operated from Stoke and continued for a number of years with some success. Seen here however, is Buxton-based class 104 set in charge of the 'Re-Opening Special', passing Milton Station on 25 February 1984.

One of my favourite photographs in this area is this one taken from the A53 bridge at Milton. The train, consisting of HJV hoppers, is the afternoon BIS Oakamoor sand quarry to Pilkington Glass Company's factory in St Helens. Class 25s, 25080 and 25195 head the train towards Stoke, passing Buller's ceramic insulator factory, on 11 March 1985.

The passage of 22 years has changed the above scene quite dramatically. Bullers' factory has closed and the site is now occupied by a new housing development. The track, although still in place and is just visible in the photograph, is now returning to nature. Hopefully, if negotiations over the re-use of this line are successful, stone trains from Cauldon Lowe Quarry, or even sand from Oakamoor, may appear once again.

By early 1987, the ubiquitous HJV/HTV hopper wagons, which normally worked the British Industrial Sand trains from Oakamoor, were replaced by their own 37.7 tonne PAA hoppers built by W.H. Davies of Longwith Junction. Seen here, near Endon on 13 May 1987, class 20s 20060 and 20113 amble towards Leekbrook with a rake of 18 PAAs.

A slight detour from its normal route takes class 120 DMU through Wall Grange, towards Leekbrook Junction, whilst working the 1040 Stoke-Cheddleton 'Churnetrail' service on 8 May 1984.

Unusual motive power appeared on the Cauldon Lowe ballast train on 25 March 1987 in the form of class 31/2 31210. The train, after leaving Leekbrook Junction, is seen here passing the former Wall Grange Station. The tower appearing in the skyline is part of the old St Edwards Mental Hospital at Cheddleton, now integrated with a prestigious new housing development.

On a warm and sunny afternoon in late May 1988 class 47, 47213 leaves Leekbrook Junction and heads on to the Stoke line with a train of railway ballast from Cauldon Lowe quarry.

A busy scene at Leekbrook Junction on 9 October 1985 with signalman Ken Faulkner accepting the Oakamoor-Leekbrook Junction single line staff from the driver of 20052 and 20215, which had just arrived from the sand quarry. The train stands on the original Churnet Valley Line, which ran for 27 miles between North Rode, just south of Macclesfield, to Uttoxeter. The line was opened throughout in 1849 and the Stoke line to Leek connected here in 1867.

Signalman Ken Faulkner at work in Leekbrook Junction signal box on 9 October 1985. The box is classic McKenzie & Holland, built for the North Staffordshire Railway Company in 1872, with a 40-lever frame. As with all the signal boxes I have had the privilege to visit-they were always immaculately and proudly kept by the signalmen.

Having run around its train at Leekbrook the driver of 20215 and 20052 collects the single line token for Milton Junction on 9 October 1985. The line to the right of the picture is to Cheddleton and Oakamoor, with the Stoke line to the left. The Cauldon Lowe branch enters behind and to the right of the bracket signal.

Signalman Eddie Hamilton holds one of the last 'Leekbrook JN–Milton JN' single line tokens to be issued before Milton Junction signal box was abolished in the summer of 1987.

During the end of February 1983 Cheddleton Station is pictured during a quite period in its development as the operating centre of the North Staffordshire Railway Company (1978) Ltd. Built in 1849, in the Jacobean style, the station has, over the last 25 years, undergone some major improvements to become the headquarters and principal station of the Churnet Valley Railway.

A year earlier in February 1982, this view of the Cheddleton site shows the former Elton Crossing signal box, which was acquired by the railway in 1978 and rebuilt here the following year. The line in 1982 was still under the ownership of British Rail and although tantalisingly close, the heritage railway had no running rights. Twenty-six years were to pass before, in 1998, they were able to make that vital connection and once more operate steam trains down the valley.

The former goods yard at Cheddleton Station is by February 1983, being used for restoration work and storage of rolling stock. In this view, the railway's self-propelled crane is busy moving equipment around. Built in 1972 by Smith of Rodley, Leeds the crane has a lifting capacity of 7 tons. It arrived at Cheddleton in March 1982 in full working order and was put to use straight away.

Prior to the Cheddleton engine shed being built, restoration work on locomotives was carried out in the open or in makeshift shelters as seen in this view taken in February 1983. In the foreground is the boiler from 4F 0-6-0 No 44422 with the frame and wheels standing to its left.

Situated at the end of the existing line in the Churnet Valley are the Oakamoor sand quarry sidings of British Industrial Sand Ltd. This picture taken on 30 August 1988 shows the conveyor-fed sand loader. The track leading into the foreground runs to the loco shed which houses the company's own Yorkshire 0-4-0 diesel shunters, 'Brightside' and 'Cammel'.

Relief driver Lionel Shaw and shunter Rex Taft pose for the camera at Oakamoor on 30 August 1988 whilst the last rail borne consignment of sand is loaded into BIS Company's PAA hoppers. Most of the shunting operations at Oakamoor were carried out by Yorkshire Engine Company's 0-4-0 shunter 'Brightside' illustrated here.

The single-road engine shed at Oakamoor housed both of the 0-4-0 shunters and was equipped with an inspection pit for maintenance work. Standing in the shed on 30 August 1988 is 'Cammel'.

The last day of rail operations from British Industrial Sand at Oakamoor was 30 August 1988. The incoming empty PAAs were booked as the 12.16pm from Stoke behind 20020 and 20132. The loaded train is seen here at Oakamoor sidings later in the afternoon ready to depart. The previous few weeks saw the daily-booked workings reducing to only once or twice per week as BIS gradually transferred their Staffordshire output to road transport. The track seen in the right foreground is all that remains of the original Churnet Valley Line which now terminates just short of the 490yard Oakamoor Tunnel. The site is now the southern extremity of the Churnet Valley Railway (1998) plc and currently used to store items of rolling stock. There are plans in the future to extend the heritage railway to here, from its current terminus at Froghall.

On the 30 August 1988, for the very last time, an Oakamoor to St Helens sand train reaches Leekbrook Junction. The second man leans out of the cab of 20020 to hand over the single line staff to signalman Eddie Hamilton.

One of the regular drivers who has worked this line for a number of years, holds the 'Leekbrook Jct-Oakamoor BIS Sdgs' single line staff for the last time on 30 August 1988.

The light railway known as the 'Leek, Cauldon Lowe & Waterhouses Railway' opened to Waterhouses on 1 July 1905. From Leekbrook, the line is 9.3 miles in length and although built under the Light Railways Act 1896 it was a quite a feat of engineering, severely graded (1 in 40 in places) and involved the construction of 15 embankments, 25 bridges, 38 culverts and 14 cuttings. Although its passenger services ceased in 1935, it continued in use for freight only and in later years, stone trains from Cauldon Lowe.

The stone and ballast traffic ceased in 1989 and today the line remains in a mothballed condition – still connected at Leekbrook – through to Cauldon Lowe Quarry. Its fate however remains uncertain.

By the time this picture was taken in 1987, stone traffic from the quarry was very infrequent. Seen here at Ipstones on 25 March 1987, unusual motive power for this line is 31210, descending the 1 in 59 to 1 in 40 gradients all the way to Leekbrook Junction, with a train of railway ballast.

At the end of January 1981, I had the privilege to meet the now late Doug Blackhurst, Chairman of Belle Engineering Ltd, Sheen. He had very kindly arranged for me take some photographs of his private railway. Doug had just completed building a third-scale replica of one of the Leek & Manifold Valley Light Railway locomotives, Kitson 2-6-4T 'JB Earle'. In this scene, Doug Blackhurst is justly proud as he stands by his magnificent engine.

On a cold January morning in 1981, Doug Blackhurst's replica Leek & Manifold Valley Light Railway 'JB Earle' steams past the camera, with Doug at the throttle, whilst climbing the steep gradient on his substantial ten and a quater inch gauge line at Sheen.

On 21 June 1987 the Hulme End terminus of the former Leek & Manifold Valley Light Railway (L&MVLR) once again became a working railway station when Doug Blackhurst's 10¹⁄₄-inch gauge 2-6-4T steam locomotive 'JB Earle' brought steam trains back to the Manifold Valley for a number of charity-day specials. Seen here at Hulme End are the temporary track, siding and signals. In the background are the original L&MVLR station building and engine shed, which are preserved and maintained as a visitor centre by Staffordshire County Council.

With safety valves lifting, Doug Blackhurst's third-scale replica 'JB Earle' clatters along the original L&MVLR track bed between Hulme End and Ecton with four well-patronised carriages. The temporary track was laid especially for the charity event held at Hulme End. Unfortunately, these charity steam specials came to an abrupt end when 'JB Earle' was involved in a serious derailment whilst working one of these specials.

4. STONE – KIDSGROVE – KENT GREEN

This part of the North Staffordshire railway network is generally regarded as the 'Main Line' and it exists almost intact to this day. It was built by the North Staffordshire Railway Company, opening in stages from 17 April 1848 to 18 June 1849. When it was completed, the line ran for just over 30 miles from Norton Bridge, (part of the Grand Junction Railway's main line between Birmingham and Warrington) via Stone, Barlaston, Stoke-on-Trent, Etruria,

Longport, Kidsgrove and Congleton, through to Macclesfield.

This chapter includes views of the railway between Stone and the north Staffordshire/south Cheshire border at Kent Green. Although the line remains largely as it was built 160 years ago, various items of the railways' infrastructure disappeared following a range of 'modernisation' schemes during the 1980s and more recently the 2002 West Coast Mainline Upgrade.

A view of the junction Station at Stone showing the line to Colwich passing to the right of the station building. No platforms exist now to serve this line but at the extreme left of the picture can be seen the footbridge to the remaining platforms for trains directly to Stoke and Stafford, via Norton Bridge. The building in the middle-right of the picture is the original NSR goods shed. When this picture was taken on 31 August 1986, the old water tower and crane were still in place at the end of the Down platform.

With its ornate bargeboards, typical of North Staffordshire Railways design, Meaford Crossing signal box was situated on the Colwich line just south of the station. The box was opened in 1880 and lasted until 2002 when it was demolished during the West Coast Mainline Upgrade.

Another view of Meaford Crossing signal box, this time taken from the Up side of the line. Interestingly, when this picture was taken on 31 August 1986, it appears that some remedial work had been done to the tiled roof by covering it with felt.

Whitebridge Crossing Keeper's house is situated just to the north of Stone station and although it is a Grade 2 listed building it is currently unoccupied and in a poor state of repair. 12 March 1991.

Whitebridge Crossing protected the railway from occasional traffic, pedestrians and animals using the unclassified Rightbridge Lane to Mount Road. Warning lights attached to the crossing gates were oil lit throughout and this picture shows Leading Railman Harold Brough re-filling its two lamps with paraffin. 12 March 1991.

The crossing gates were interlocked and could not be opened until the Meaford Crossing signalman released its locking mechanism. On 12 March 1991, Harold Brough is at the ground frame and about to unlock the crossing gates for traffic to cross safely. The crossing closed to traffic and pedestrians during late 1991, ahead of a new road bridge built to connect with a new housing development.

Barlaston signal box came into use along with the station in 1849 and continued with its original wheel-operated crossing gates right up to its closure in 1985. Note the extended bay window.

During the nineteen eighties, a number of special trains worked the Venice Simplon Orient Express Pullman stock into the Stoke area. Seen here on 21 March 1984, class 86/2 86206 'City of Stoke-on-Trent' rushes through Barlaston station with a charter from London to Stoke-on-Trent.

One of the private roads into the Wedgwood factory at Barlaston crossed the main line at Wedgwood Station. It had its own crossing keeper to operate the manually operated gates, which continued right up to being replaced with CCTV controlled barriers in 2002. Seen here on 31 March 1989 is the crossing keeper closing the gates for a 'Wedgwood' charter train. The crossing keeper's house is seen in the background.

Wedgwood Station (or halt, as it became in later years) opened in the 1950s and during the following 20 years became a busy station as Wedgwood factory workers travelled by train to its rural location. In this picture the diminutive booking office, although not in use, was still standing on 31 March 1989.

On 31 March 1989 The Venice Simplon Orient Express arrives at Wedgwood Station behind 86/2 86236, 'Josiah Wedgwood', whilst working a special charter to the factory from London. The train went on to Cockshute Sidings Stoke to turn in readiness for the return working.

The platforms and shelters at Wedgwood Station were constructed entirely from wood and this view clearly shows the wooden decking to the platforms. Local people are seen here obviously enjoying the spectacle of such a luxury train slightly off its normal route!

Kerr Stuart Locomotive Works

From the late nineteen hundreds Stoke had a tradition of railway locomotive, carriage and wagon manufacture. In addition to the North Staffordshire Railway Company's locomotive and carriage works at Stoke there was another world famous company, which began building locomotives in the town, namely Kerr, Stuart & Co.

The business started in Glasgow Scotland, in 1883 but during this time they were only acting as agents ordering locomotives from established manufacturers. However they purchased the Stoke-based Hartley, Arnoux and Fanning in 1892 and moved into the California Works at Whieldon Road to begin building all their own locomotives. Hartley, Arnoux and Fanning had already been building railway and tramway plant but this side of their business was sold to Dick Kerr & Co in Preston.

Some 1500 locomotives were constructed at the California Works and exported all around the world until manufacture ceased in 1930, the company having gone bankrupt. During this year the firm's designs and spare parts were bought by the Hunslet Engine Company in Leeds and some Kerr Stuart-design locomotives went on to be built by W.G Bagnall at their Stafford factory. Under new ownership the Kerr Stuart works then became Brookfield Foundry, which started a long association with The Admiralty to manufacture turrets for warships. Thereafter the foundry gradually became inactive and rail traffic ceased in about 1962. By 1982 Brookfield Foundry went into liquidation and the site closed the following year. However, railway wagon building and repair continues to this day at the nearby Marcroft Engineering works situated off Whieldon Road, Stoke.

A view of Brookfield Foundry, during early 1981, looking northwest towards the Whieldon Road entrance. Even at this late date, the entire site retained its original 'cobble' yards.

Brookfield Foundry looking south, with railway tracks still visible in the work's yard. March 1981.

This view shows the main erecting shop at Brookfield Foundry, looking towards Stoke. The main line from Stoke to Norton Bridge passes to the right of the picture. March 1981.

This photograph, taken at Brookfield Foundry in March 1981, shows a locomotive with strong local links and during its career did not move out of the area. The design is an unusual one, with outside valve gear and a very small saddle tank, reminiscent of Kerr Stuart's narrow gauge designs. Delivered new in 1926 to the Stoke-on-Trent Corporation's gas works at Etruria, Stoke-on-Trent, number 4388 was the first locomotive employed there. It also shunted coal wagons at the NSR Etruria yard, remaining at Etruria until 7 July 1950 when it returned to its place of manufacture, then Brookfield Foundry, as a works shunter.

The other locomotive that survived at the Brookfield Foundry was Bagnall 0-6-0PT No 2613, built in 1940. When the foundry went into liquidation both locomotives went for auction. No 4388 was purchased privately and transferred to the Foxfield Railway Society on 13 February 1983 and subsequently restored at the Crewe Heritage Centre. No 2613 was also restored to working order and named "Brookfield" and now carries a blue livery. Following numerous visits to steam railways around the UK it can now be found at the Mangapps Railway Museum in Essex. Both locomotives are seen here outside the old locomotive erecting shop at Brookfield Foundry in March 1981.

Kerr Stuart and latterly Brookfield Foundry had a direct rail connection with the Stoke line just south of Stoke Junction. The alignment, seen here, leads out from bottom left of the picture. The original cast iron gate pillars are also visible centre left. The 08 shunter passing the site is heading towards Marcroft Engineering Ltd.

Typical motive power on the English China Clay trains during this period and heading south past Whieldon Grove is 45068 with a rake of empty Tiger Rail bogie hoppers, possibly working right through to Cornwall.

1982 witnessed some changes to the skyline at Glebe Street when developers demolished a substantial section of the Station goods sheds to make way for a new commercial warehouse and offices for Swift Electronics. This view taken in June that year shows the demolition work well under way.

During the demolition of the goods sheds, contractors had to decide on how to dispose of two box vans, which had been 'marooned' (with no rail connection) inside one of the sheds. The vans were historically important items being LMS 1930s – built 12-ton box vans. Eventually the Foxfield Railway Society rescued both vans and found them a new home at Blythe Bridge.

The notoriously low railway bridge at Glebe Street claimed many a top deck from local PMT double deck buses. Seen here in late November 1984 the Crewe wiring train is removing some of the overhead equipment as Stoke North Yard progressively closed down.

China clay traffic to the English China Clay plant at Cliff Vale was normally handled by class 45 and 46 locos, but during the miners' industrial action, a surplus of class 56s became available to work this traffic. Class 56s continued working ECC trains into Stoke for some years after this. Seen here leaving Stoke North Yard on 29 October 1984, 56094 heads south with a rake of 'empty' Tiger Rail bogies.

During the 1970s and 80s, Stoke-on-Trent enjoyed a frequent rail service to Stafford and Manchester. Class 304 EMUs worked most of the diagrams but occasionally class 310s would make an appearance. On 30 April 1984 310 074 is seen here leaving Stoke Station with a mid-day Manchester-Stafford service.

Class 40s were regular performers in north Staffordshire and on a cold and wet 17 October 1984, 40015 'Aquitania', is seen passing over the 'arches' as it approaches Stoke North Yard with a Cauldon Lowe Quarry-Cockshute Sidings ballast train.

On 21 March 1985 class 45s were back on the English China Clay trains and on this particular day 45072 was in charge. Normally the train would have avoided the station through Stoke North Yard but by this time, the yard had closed.

This picture, taken in June 1984, shows more unusual motive power for the English China Clay trains. On this occasion class 31/1 31176 is the locomotive of choice as it is seen passing through Stoke Yard with a rake of Tiger Rail bogies from Cliffe Vale to Bescot.

A Stoke-based 08 shunter undertook movements of new or refurbished wagons, to and from Marcroft Engineering's wagon works at Whieldon Road. On 6 April 1982, 08329 is seen just entering Stoke Station with two of Marcroft's products.

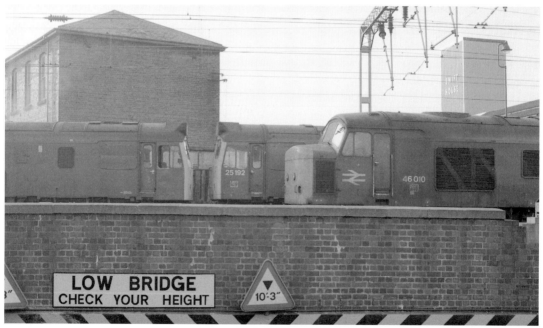

Glebe Street Bridge, situated just south of Stoke Station, was a good vantage point for 'spotting' since trains entering or leaving Stoke yard could be held on signals and invariably stopped on the bridge. These next three pictures show the variety of motive power to be seen at Stoke during the 1980s. On 1 December 1983, Class 46010 is working the English China Clay 'empties' from Cliffe Vale and 25079 and 25192 are waiting to head north with the Oakamoor-St Helens sand train.

On 11 September 1983, 20075 and 20113 wait at signals to pass through Stoke Yard with five brake vans to Cockshute Sidings.

The summer of 1984 saw class 58s making appearances on the Scunthorpe–Shelton Bar steel works trains and seen here is 58014 with a mid day return working. Waiting to head north is 25089 with an Oakamoor to Longport sand train.

Early 1984 saw the run down of Stoke North Yard as freight traffic in the area diminished. This was the scene on 4 December 1984 when most of the sidings had already been lifted and Stoke North Yard signal box closed. It was demolished shortly after this picture was taken.

On 16 October 1984, just prior to the remaining tracks being lifted, 40015 'Aquitania' passes through Stoke yard on its way to Cockshute Sidings. Some of the sidings here had already gone as evidenced in the foreground.

Stoke Station building itself has changed very little over the years and this view, looking north on 6 April 1982, shows a class 310 EMU 310089 working an afternoon Manchester-Stafford train.

The 1984 summer timetable included a number of cross-country services worked by InterCity 125 trains calling at Stoke. The first of these trains, the 1642 Manchester-Plymouth, is seen here departing Stoke Station on 14 May 1984.

With the start of the 1985/86 timetable on Monday 13 May, InterCity launched a number of new Pullman services on its principal business routes. Twenty services were involved, 10 on the London–Manchester corridor, 8 on the Liverpool services and one train each way between Kings Cross and West Yorkshire. Seen here at Stoke Station on 13 May 1985, John Birkin, Lord Mayor of Stoke-on-Trent, flags away the first of the new Pullman trains to London on the first day of the new timetable.

Class 58 locomotives started to appear on the Scunthorpe–Shelton Bar steel trains during 1984. Heading north towards Shelton Bar, 58002 is seen with one of these trains on 5 December 1984.

Apart from the china clay traffic class 46s made occasional appearances at Stoke with trains from Longport or Cockshute Sidings. On 14 April 1982 46028 heads south past Stoke Power Box with an unidentified, train of Railfreight SPAs.

The goods bay at the north end of platform one at Stoke was used occasionally to stable locomotives. One such occasion was 15 October 1984 when a very tidy looking 40152 sits in the bay waiting for its next turn. This area is now a taxi rank.

An interesting visitor to the Stoke area, class 50 50027 'Lion' departs from Stoke station with the A1 Tours 'Settle and Carlisle Land Cruise' on 29 August 1984. Starting from Birmingham, the rail tour was hauled by the class 50 to Preston, where 40122/D200 took over for the remainder of the trip.

On 23 May 1987, another enthusiasts' special calls at Stoke Station, this time with 40122/D200, drawing into platform 1 with the 1Z37 'Gwent Valley Explorer' rail tour from Crewe to Newport, Barry Island and Cardiff.

On 22 October 1985 the morning Oakamoor to Longport sand train was shunting in Stoke when it crashed through buffers and demolished the retaining wall above the Stoke–Shelton main road. This was the scene mid day with the Crewe Breakdown Train in attendance. Class 25/1 No 25058 (CD) leans into the road with class 25/2 No 25213 (CD) behind. Miraculously no one was hurt in the incident.

Just north of Stoke Station, in what used to be the original NSR carriage sidings, 08737 shunts a permanent way train on 28 November 1987. These sidings are still in use today, mainly for permanent way stock.

Cockshute Sidings

Cockshute railway sidings were situated approximately half a mile to the north of Stoke Station and comprised an extensive web of sidings on the east side of the main line and to the western side were carriage/ EMU sidings, locomotive stabling tracks and a three-road shed. The shed in fact was built in 1957 as a maintenance depot for the fleet of DMUs that had taken over local steam hauled passenger workings. The following photographs give an indication of how Cockshute Sidings looked and operated in the 1980s.

A melancholy view of Cockshute Sidings signal box, taken on 3 February 1986 when it was being stripped ready for demolition. However, it stood in this condition until the middle of 1987, the whole area being in a state of dereliction with most of the track already cut up and cleared from the site. The massive structure in the distance is the Etruria Gas Works waterless gasholder, said to be one of the largest of its type in the country.

Cockshute Sidings signal box in happier times with 25245 passing on the main line with a welded rail train. Picture taken in May 1985.

Another view of the eastern side sidings, taken on 12 April 1984, with two roads occupied by condemned DMU sets. The large structure on the right of the picture is Twyfords Sanitary Ware Company's Etruria factory.

The Venice Simplon Orient Express Pullmans visited Stoke-on-Trent on 21 March 1984 with a high-end charter from London Euston, hauled by 86206 'City of Stoke-on-Trent'. Whilst at Stoke the train was stabled for most of the time at Cockshute Carriage Sidings. Seen here at the sidings, the luxury train attracted quite a bit of attention from members of the public.

During the 1980s Cockshute Sidings were host to various condemned locos, DMUs and items of passenger stock. In this view taken on 13 June 1984, a class 506 EMU set No M59408M was at the head of a long formation waiting to be taken for scrap. It was unusual to see class 506 units in the Stoke area (even condemned sets) since they were unique to the Manchester 1500v DC overhead system, working the Manchester-Hadfield services. The class was withdrawn altogether on 17 November 1984 when the line converted to 25Kv AC and worked by class 303 sets.

Sunday evenings saw several sets of Class 304 EMUs at Cockshute Carriage Sidings ready for the following week's work on the Manchester-Stoke-Stafford services. On 26 April 1987, four of the class are stabled here over the weekend.

Although there were carriage-washing facilities in the old DMU shed at Cockshute Sidings, EMU sets could not access this facility because the overhead supply finished at the entrance road. However, two bays were created outside for servicing and washing the EMUs. For obvious safety reasons the overhead lines were curtailed at the start of the two bays and the Units were shunted in and out as required. Sets 304040 and 304011 are seen in the washing bays on 26 April 1987.

Another line-up of condemned AC electric locos at Cockshute sidings, photographed on 13 June 1984. Left to right, 83008; 83005; 83007; 83010; 83002; 82006; 82004 and 83013.

Taken on the same day, a close up of 83013 shows the amount of equipment removed, including pantograph, insulators and windows.

Locomotives entering or leaving Cockshute shed and stabling roads had to negotiate a severe gradient which is clearly shown in this picture taken on 30 May 1987. Class 47/5, 47544 rushes north with an afternoon Birmingham-Manchester service.

Seen here on 18 September 1984, storming out of Cockshute shed roads, 37008 makes quite an effort hauling dead class 40, 40118 up the steep grade to join the main line. (Peter Rawlins).

Apart from the DMU shed and water tower, another structure at Cockshute sidings was the shunters' cabin/messroom, which dated from the 1950s. Seen here on 30 May 1987 it still had two blackboards on the wall with 'British Railways' totems and an improvised bench seat made from bricks topped with a sleeper!

A typical weekend scene at the locomotive stabling point at Cockshute sidings. In this view taken on 11 August 1984 were resident locos, left to right, 40079; 40056; 20182 and 20199.

On the evening of 11 August 1984 at Cockshute sidings, looking northeast, are seen 20182; 40079; 47350 and 47202. The water tower and DMU shed are visible just behind the class 47s.

A few weeks later another view of Cockshute stabling point shows 20199 (paired with 20182) and 40118 coupled to 37008. This picture was taken on 15 September 1984.

This is a view of Cockshute DMU shed taken on 26 April 1987 from the north end at Shelton New Road. The shed, never fully enclosed, was open to the elements at both ends.

An unusual visitor arrived at Cockshute sidings on 25 May 1987 in the form of a class 56 locomotive. Seen here inside the shed, 56061 looks in ex-works condition.

This picture shows the south end of Cockshute DMU shed on 30 May 1987 with the resident shunter, 08613, just visible inside.

On 21 October 1990, the view had completely changed. The sidings had closed, track gave way to tarmac for a car park and the old shed had now become a new development for light industrial units.

On the west side of the mainline, at Cliffe Vale, English China Clay Ltd (ECC) built their new works to process raw Cornish clay for the local pottery industry. Up to the early 1980s, china clay travelled to Stoke in 13ton UCV china clay wagons, which then had to be manually offloaded. In 1982, when ECC had opened its new facility at Cliffe Vale, the clay was delivered directly utilising a fleet of new 56.3ton bogie PBA 'Clayhops', built in France by Fauvet Giril and leased to ECC from Tiger Rail Leasing Ltd. The ECC plant is just visible above class 45, 45005, which had recently arrived with its train. The line to the extreme right leads into Cockshute stabling point.

On 13 August 1984, 56064 was in charge of the daily ECC 'Tigers' and is seen here at Cliffe Vale waiting to depart. The numbered posts act as a reference point to enable the driver to position each wagon into the discharge zone, which is visible at the rear of the train. (Peter Rawlins)

Heading north from Stoke the next station is Etruria. An interesting station in that it had only island platforms, accessed by a single flight of steps from the main A53 Newcastle-Hanley road. Two tracks ran either side of the island, providing Up and Down fast/slow lines. On 14 March 1985, 25262 passed through the station with a Glasgow-Derby ECS working.

Losing its usual quantity of sand, the Oakamoor-St Helens sand train heads through Etruria on 14 March 1985 with 25256 and 25316 in charge.

On 14 March 1985, a class 33 makes an unexpected appearance at Etruria. 33022 is seen here heading north with a condemned class 304 EMU, 304025.

The following year Etruria witnessed two of the class, No's 33051 and 33062, providing the motive power for an enthusiast special the 'Wirral Witherins' rail tour on a very cold and wet 18 January 1986.

Looking north towards the main A53 bridge at Etruria on 14 March 1985, class 120 DMU departs the station with the 1320 Derby-Crewe service. Unfortunately, passenger services from Etruria were to last only another ten years. The station closed altogether on 30 September 2005.

In addition to the hourly Crewe-Derby trains, Etruria enjoyed frequent Stafford-Manchester, and Stoke-Macclesfield services. The island platform can be clearly seen in this view as EMU, class 304 043 arrives with the 1348 Stafford-Manchester. 14 March 1985.

On 17 April 1988, 37078 accelerates southbound away from Etruria with an engineers' spoil train. By this date class 37s were becoming frequent visitors to the area, particularly on the Bescot-Longport petroleum tanks for Carless Petroleum works at Bradwell.

Shortly after leaving Wolstanton Colliery exchange sidings, 40004 thunders towards Longport with a northbound coal train, seen here on 3 February 1983.

Longport

Longport was an important part of the north Staffordshire's railway network. It had extensive sidings on both sides of the main line and transhipment sheds (still in use in the 1980s) and up to 1967 was a busy junction with the branch line to Pinnox Junction and the Potteries Loop Line. The branch at that time was used frequently as a diversionary route to Kidsgrove during the construction of the new electrified line that would avoid Harecastle Tunnel. These next few pictures illustrate the railway as it looked during the 1980s and the varied railway movements in and around Longport.

Longport station, with its almost Gothic style buildings, was a busy station and when this picture was taken it had well kept waiting rooms, toilets, platform seats and was also fully staffed. The date is Sunday 6 November 1983 and the 2-car DMU is working a shuttle service between Stoke Station and Kidsgrove whilst weekend engineering work was undertaken. Although the station building is Grade 2 listed it is now completely boarded up and out of use and has become merely an un-staffed halt.

On a dull 22 May 1985, 25080 heads north through Longport station with a train of railway ballast from Cauldon Lowe Low Quarry.

A view of the sidings situated on the west side of the main line, taken on 2 June 1986. Class 20s 20107 and 20116 were just about to depart with a Longport-St Helens sand train, which had been brought in earlier from Oakamoor.

A view of the southern end of Longport sidings (west), taken on 6 November 1983, shows the stop blocks, a single 20ton brake van and a rake of Departmental ZDVs. The large building on the right is part of Billington & Newton Ltd's Foundry, which cast ships propellers and other marine parts. That site was cleared a few years after this picture was taken and is now occupied by a modern distribution warehouse. The sidings remain, derelict and overgrown.

On 16 April 1985 20096 and 20162 wait in Longport sidings after bringing in a sand train from BIS Oakamoor. Two unidentified 20s are in the east yard along with several Ferrywagon bogies.

On 23 July 1985 class 20s, 20071 and 20045 stand beside Longport Junction signal box waiting to head onto the main line with a Longport-St Helens sand train. This particular box, built to an LMS design, opened in 1939, probably due to the increased traffic during the war effort. It replaced an earlier 19th century NSR box and was itself demolished on 27 May 2002 as part of the West Coast Main Line Upgrade works.

Late evening at Longport sidings on 7 November 1984 and the yard lights and descending fog make a very atmospheric picture of 40168 as it waits to depart with a Longport-Falkland Junction scrap train. (Peter Rawlins).

On 23 October 1985 a class 58, 58020 heads north through Longport Station with a Toton-Garston MGR. The DMU in platform 1 is an unidentified Crewe-Derby service.

On a cold but sunny 3 February 1983, 47290 heads south past Longport goods shed, with its MGR 'empties' to Grange Junction and Wolstanton Colliery exchange sidings. The row of houses seen in the background, behind the brake van, formed part of the neat little village of Longbridge Hayes. The whole of the village area is now an industrial estate and scrap recycling plant.

A weekend possession at Longport to lay new continuously welded rail sees a ballast train of ZEV 'Catfish' wagons and vacuum only ZUV 'Shark' having just made a pass over the Down line on Sunday 11 October 1987.

In order to create the continuously welded rail, the joints are 'Thermit welded' by a spectacular process of firing up a pyrotechnic mixture of powdered steel and magnesium into the gap between the rail ends. The finished weld is then ground-off to provide a perfect running surface. Sunday 11 October 1987.

On Sunday 18 October 1987 the Up line at Longport had permanent way work in progress and seen here running through the station is ZUV 'Shark' with its blades down distributing the new ballast.

This is a view of Longport goods sheds sidings taken in April 1988 with the resident shunter stabled for the weekend. The track in the foreground leads from the west sidings past the signal box and down to Bradwell sidings and the Carless chemical works. The station is just behind the white-roofed building.

Inside the main trans-shipment shed at Longport on 6 February 1987 showing its international connections. Various 54tonne International Ferry Wagons (TOPS code IPB) in VTG and Scunthorpe Rolling Mill liveries are seen in the four-road shed. At this time, some of these vehicles brought in large quantities of steel coil for local engineering companies.

A long way from its home on the DB railway in Germany, 'Cargowagon' IBP stands in Longport yard ready for its return journey. These bulk carriers can carry 54tonnes of cargo, which are capable of very rapid loading and unloading via three large opening side panels, giving access to one third of the vehicle at a time. 6 February 1987.

On 6 February 1987, 47324 stands at the head shunt, by Longport goods shed, whilst waiting to run round its train for Bescot.

AC electric 85040 draws out of Longport sidings on 16 June 1982 with a Longport-Bescot mixed freight.

It is summer 1985 and a rake of bogie bolsters (BDAs) ran into the head shunt stop blocks. Two of the bogies derailed, promptly demolishing the rear wall of Longport station's platform 1 and pushing over approx 10 metres of concrete platform decking onto the Up running line. Fortunately, no one was injured in the incident but the line remained closed for most of the day. (Peter Rawlins)

Another view of the incident at Longport with unidentified class 31 in charge of the Crewe Breakdown Train. Summer 1985. (Peter Rawlins)

Having already made a trip down to Carless Petroleum Company's sidings at Bradwell to pick up their tank wagons, Longport shunter 08921 propels them into the 'Pinnox Branch' sidings at Longport. May 1989.

The 'Pinnox Branch' sidings were quite extensive as can be seen in this view taken in April 1984. The Pinnox Branch itself, before closure in 1968, swung around to the right in this picture and on past the southern end of Westport Lake and up to Pinnox Junction where it connected with the Potteries Loop line to Tunstall. The unidentified class 45, had just set back with a train of condemned DMU sets bound for Cockshute Sidings. The train had made a stop here because a 'hot box' in one of the units had been detected between Kidsgrove and Longport. (Peter Rawlins)

Another view of the 'Pinnox Branch' sidings taken in May 1984, this time with a trio of class 25s at work. On the left is 25195 with a ballast train and 25285 and 25245 are light engines having recently arrived with an Oakamoor sand train. (Peter Rawlins)

On 9 October 1987, 47590 'Thomas Telford' heads out of the 'Pinnox' sidings with a Longport-Bescot mixed freight. Resident shunter, 08913, is busy working in the sidings. (Peter Rawlins)

Once the Carless tanks were assembled in 'Pinnox' sidings the booked locomotive, on this occasion Petroleum sub-Sector class 37, 37676 would attach ready for the journey to Bescot. The duty shunter Bob Watts speaks to the driver before departure.

At this time, there was a lot of activity at Lonport and with continual shunter duties required, a permanent shunter's cabin on the 'Pinnox' side was available for staff. Bob Watts, a main member of the shunting team at Longport, stands by the train of Carless tanks he had just assembled at 'Pinnox' sidings.

Throughout most of the summer of 1985, major changes took place during the Crewe Remodelling work. Some of this involved singling the line between Radway Green and North Stafford Junction at Crewe. BR required the lifted track to be stored and dismantled and decided that the mothballed sidings at Chatterley Valley were ideal. The 'sidings' were in fact the remains of the old NSR main line, left in place when the Harecastle Diversion Line opened in 1967. In this picture, taken on 12 June 1985, departmental class 97, 97406 (40135), propels a train of track panels into the temporary 'sidings' at Chatterley Valley. Above the train, the Diversion line swings to the left. The structure appearing above the trees to the left is what remains of the old Chatterley Ironworks.

On the same day, 12 June 1985, 97406 stands in Chatterley Valley as track, redundant from the Crewe branch, is off loaded by road crane before dismantling by contractors. The train is standing on what was the old Up line and the line nearest the camera was the access road to sidings of the former Goldendale Ironworks.

During October 1988, the railway landscape in Chatterley Valley was to undergo further changes as a coal loading plant, built to dispose of coal brought in by road from an opencast site near Silverdale, nears completion. The line in the foreground is the main (Diversion Line) to Kidsgrove. The new track-bed to the coal loader, is clearly visible, with hardcore already laid.

The scene had changed dramatically on 19 July 1989, when this picture was taken at Chatterley Valley Coal Disposal site. New rail connections into the loading area are complete and the loader had commenced operations. Alongside the main line, class 20s, 20013 and 20087 are running round, having just brought in one of the first MGR trains to this facility. The scene now is completely changed and although the rail connections remain but overgrown, the coal loader and associated site has gone, making way for the A500 connection to the A50 at Sandyford. The horizon is now dominated by bridges connected with this major road scheme.

From Chatterley the line is steeply graded. It then levels just before Bathpool Park and then descends past Bathpool through the new Harecastle Tunnel and into Kidsgrove. Seen here on 13 March 1983, 47453 storms up the bank towards Peacocks Hay, with the 1000 Euston-Manchester.

Having made the climb from Kidsgrove, 47455 'drags' 86251 'The Birmingham Post' together with the 1447 Manchester-Euston through Bathpool Park, on 13 February 1983.

On 6 March 1983, 40012 'Auriol' is in charge of 86250 'The Glasgow Herald' and the 1447 Manchester-Euston, as it makes its way under Peacocks Hay bridge.

On a sunny 13 May 1984, 47479 is in charge of 86236 and the 1150 Euston-Manchester Piccadilly as it descends the bank through Bathpool Park.

Just breasting the top of the grade at Bathpool Park, 37684 accelerates away with a rake of empty coaching stock to Derby on 11 September 1985. (Peter Rawlins).

A sylvan setting at Bathpool on 13 May 1984 as 47423 leaves Harecastle Tunnel with the 1425 Manchester Piccadilly-Birmingham service.

The calm of a warm summer evening is shattered by the sound of a class 40 in full song as 40155 bursts out of Harecastle Tunnel to climb Bathpool bank, en route to Stoke. The train is working the return leg of a BR Staff club "Stoke to Blaenau Ffestiniog" excursion on 5 August 1984. (Peter Rawlins).

Only seconds after leaving Harecastle Tunnel 86216 'Meteor' hurtles over the junction crossing at Kidsgrove Central with the 1350 Euston-Manchester on 26 July 1983. For some reason, which was never made clear, the signal box name-board became "Kidsgrove", as seen in this picture. It lasted for only a matter of weeks and then mysteriously reverted to Kidsgrove Central.

On 18 September 1983, with the signal box bearing its proper name, 40033 'Empress of England' rattles over the junction with 86217 'Comet' and the 1250 Euston-Manchester. The signal box opened in 1965 during the electrification of this line. It closed on 27 May 2002 as part of the West Coast Mainline Upgrade works.

Snow in the Potteries on 22 December 1985 contributed to the failure, at Stoke, of the class 304 EMU, which was working the 1340 Stafford-Manchester Piccadilly. Class 20s, numbers 20131 and 20125 formed the rescue party and the train is seen here storming into Kidsgrove Central approx 40 minutes late.

On the last day of scheduling class 120 DMUs on the Derby services, two of the class meet at Kidsgrove on 19 January 1986. The 1520 Crewe-Lincoln (right) and the 1232 Lincoln-Crewe are seen here discharging passengers at platforms 3 and 4. During the following few days class 150 'Sprinters' replaced the 120s on these diagrams.

Track replacement was the order of the day in September 1989 and seen here at Kidsgrove Central is a works train levelling ballast through the station with an unidentified Railfreight class 31.

On a Sunday in early September 1989, engineering crews had taken possession of the line through Kidsgrove. This was the second weekend of track renewal and in this view the P-way crew is manhandling lengths of rail through platform 2, while at the signal box Plasser & Theurer type 07-16 Unomatic levelling and tamping machine has just completed a pass over the newly constructed track.

As two passengers study a newly revised timetable, they are oblivious to 47041 as it rattles through Kidsgrove with an empty ballast train to Longport on 22 April 1984.

On 18 December 1984 the 1511 Stafford-Manchester Piccadilly, usually worked by a class 304 EMU, was replaced with a 2-car DMU set. The unit is seen here at Kidsgrove with Leading Railman Harold Brough checking passenger tickets as they leave the train.

On 25 October 1987, engineering operations at Longport closed the line and this required a bus service connection between Stoke and Kidsgrove stations. A class 304 EMU shuttle service provided the rail link between Manchester Piccadilly and Kidsgrove. Seen here at Kidsgrove a 304 set has just arrived with passengers being directed to the waiting buses by Harold Brough (centre).

On a rainy 27 November 1983, unusual motive power appeared on the 1425 Manchester Piccadilly-Birmingham, in the form of 'Peak' 45123 'The Lancashire Fusilier'. Seen here at Kidsgrove it is waiting for the 'Pilot' to board to operate the train 'wrong line' through to Longport.

A very 'untypical' operation occurred at Kidsgrove on 11 November 1987, when a class 304 EMU, working the 1342 Manchester Piccadilly-Stoke, was propelled into the Station for its scheduled stop by 47480 with its train the 1401 Manchester Picadilly-Birmingham. The EMU had failed at Congleton and with no refuge facilities between Congleton and Longport it was decided to push the train forward to Stoke.

In 1982 Kidsgrove still retained its goods yard at the station and passing loops situated at Liverpool Road. On Sunday 27 June 1982 class 25s, 25086 and 25140 emerge from the Down passing loop with an engineers' spoil train to work 'wrong line' through the station.

Kidsgrove's goods yard still saw activity as seen in this picture, taken on 30 December 1984. During the festive break, an engineers train is stabled in the yard together with the local coal merchants' loaders.

The goods yard office at Kidsgrove station, dating from c1849, was still in use on 29 August 1983 for transactions associated with the Land Sale Wharf which operated in the yard at that time. The wall to the right of the building is part of the Trent & Mersey Harecastle canal bridge. Note the oval LMS bridge number plate attached to the wall and the diamond shaped cast iron North Staffordshire Railway Company's' weight limits sign. All this has gone and the land consigned to housing development.

Un-seasonal cold weather at Kidsgrove on 7 April 1984 and both steam-heat 25s, 25042 and 25214 had the boilers on for a North Staffordshire Railway Company (1978) Ltd charter the 'Knotty Northern Circular' from Stoke, for a trip over the Settle and Carlisle.

Unusual working for a passenger train but this Hertfordshire Railtours' charter, the 'Midland Macedoine', was on its return working having already travelled the freight-only lines in Peak Forest and Great Rocks and on to Buxton. Class 58, 58007 is seen here passing Kidsgrove goods yard on 19 September 1984.

An immaculate 40122 (D200) rushes past Kidsgrove Liverpool Road on 31 August 1987 with a Train Tours charter, 'The Desert Songster'. The train ran from Preston and Stockport to Kensington Olympia, Exeter, Taunton, Reading and return.

During the first quarter of 1988, a number of class 50s worked a Paddington-Manchester Piccadilly throughout. Normally, the '50' would switch over at Birmingham New Street for a class 47. On 9 March 1988, 50044 in Network Southeast livery, worked through to Manchester and seen here, between Scholar Green and Kidsgrove Liverpool Road, with the 1400 Manchester Piccadilly-Paddington

When this picture was taken on 23 January 1983, the Up and Down loops were operational and were used quite often to hold freight trains for passenger workings to pass. With the decline of freight the loops were removed and scheduled freight trains no longer operate between Kidsgrove and Macclesfield. In this picture 47561 heads south with the 1443 Manchester Piccadilly-Paddington and to the rear of the train Kidsgrove Liverpool Road signal box is just visible.

This picture shows Kidsgrove Liverpool Road signal box taken On 30 December 1984. The box was opened by the NSR in 1875 to govern the web of lines at Liverpool Road (Loop Line) Junction and although boarded-up and out of use it had been closed only eight years. This happened because of open cast coal extraction at Goldenhill requiring this part of the Loop Line to remain open until August 1976 when rail-born traffic then ceased altogether.

On 7 July 1985, class 47/2, 47204 heads north over the viaduct and past Liverpool Road signal box with a ballast train. The line in the foreground is the Down passing loop, which is still in use by this date. (Peter Rawlins)

A gloomy 13 March 1983 and 40029 'Saxonia' makes light work of the 1030 Manchester Piccadilly–Birmingham train as it storms through Scholar Green.

One of the smallest signal cabins opened by the North Staffordshire Railway was Mow Cop. It was built to the NSR standard design in 1890, which had brick bases and small locking room windows. The box remained open until 27 May 2002 when it came out of use because of the West Coast Mainline Upgrade. Interestingly it was saved by a member of the public and demolition of the box was delayed until October 2002 to allow the owner to remove the box to a new location.

On 22 April 1984, 47436 thunders over the crossing at Mow Cop with the 1150 Euston Manchester.

Heading south over the crossing at Mow Cop, on 27 March 1983, is 47415 with the 1030 Manchester Piccadilly-Birmingham service.

The power is off and diesel power comes to the rescue on 3 April 1983 when 47537 hauls 86209 'City of Coventry' and the 1200 Euston-Manchester Piccadilly through Kent Green.

The two cows in the field at Kent Green are used to the sound of trains and look disinterested as a very noisy 40015 'Aquitania' tows 86213 'Lancashire Witch' and the 1447 Manchester Piccadilly-Euston on 3 April 1983.

5. HOLDITCH – SILVERDALE – MADELEY

Early in 1986, class 20s had replaced class 47 duties on the Silverdale-Ironbridge Power Station with merry-go-round trains. Locomotive problems at this time and permanent way work at Madeley Chord caused some trips to be cancelled, angering local residents when the traffic was taken by road. On 28 May 1986, rail haulage resumed with class 20s 20007 and 20047 seen at the Silverdale loader.

The NSR line into Shropshire left the Stoke-Manchester line at Newcastle Junction, Stoke. It opened fully to Market Drayton in February 1870, and there were stations at Newcastle, Silverdale, Keele, Madeley Road, Pipe Gate and Norton in Hales. A branch, connecting with this line at Apedale Junction, to Apedale, had already been constructed in 1859 and as Holditch Colliery developed, from 1912, a further connection was made at Whitebarn Junction to accommodate a line into the colliery. Passenger services operated between Stoke and Market Drayton until all scheduled passenger services, west of Silverdale, were withdrawn on 7 May 1956. A much reduced passenger service survived between Stoke and Silverdale until 1964. However, the line had a new lease of life in 1962 when it was connected to the West Coast Main Line at Madeley Chord. This allowed Stoke-Crewe traffic to be re-routed and so avoiding the new electrification work north of Stoke. On completion of the electrification the line was closed as a through route on 8 March 1966 and the track from Newcastle Junction to Brampton Sidings was lifted soon afterwards. The following pictures show the line as it remained in use for coal traffic from Holditch Colliery and Silverdale Colliery. In 1989, Holditch closed down and the track from the colliery through to Silverdale was removed. On 31 December 1998, Silverdale Colliery also closed and the line, through to Madeley, remains in a derelict state. Silverdale Station building was demolished brick by brick by a group of volunteers in 2002 and transported to the Apedale Mining Museum to be re-erected there as part of a narrow gauge feature. Unfortunately, this was not completed and the materials were used elsewhere in the museum site.

On 22 April 1982, class 25s 25208 and 25075 get to grips with a loaded coal train out of Holditch Colliery. The train seen here approaching Knutton Crossing, with the gates already opened by the guard. The train will proceed to Apedale Junction, where the locos will run round the train and continue via Silverdale to Madeley Chord where it will join the main line to Crewe.

On the inward journey to Holditch Colliery, 25075 and 25208 wait for the guard to secure the crossing gates protecting the Milehouse to Knutton road. 22 April 1982.

Seven years later, when Holditch Colliery had closed and mineral traffic ceased to operate beyond Silverdale, an 8-car DMU, chartered by The Institution of Mining Engineers, worked over the branch from Madeley Chord to Holditch Colliery. The ensemble is seen here running between Apedale Junction and Knutton Crossing on 22 October 1989.

The three dogs seen on the playing field are, I would guess, uninterested in 25075 and 25208, almost at Apedale Junction, with a train of 'empties' to Holditch Colliery. 22 April 1982. Newcastle under Lyme is in the distance to the left of the train. 22 April 1982.

At Apedale Junction, trains taking the branch to Holditch colliery ran round the train using the remaining track which once continued to Brampton Sidings and Newcastle. On 12 April 1988, class 20s, 20034 and 20147 were in charge of a coal train from Holditch, seen here having done the reverse manoeuvre and are proceeding from Apedale Junction towards Silverdale. (Peter Rawlins)

The line from Apedale Junction to Madeley Chord was steeply graded in places. In this picture taken on 18 March 1987, 47568 has already climbed from Apedale Junction with a train from Holditch Colliery and is on a short down hill stretch, to pass under the Knutton to Keele road bridge before negotiating Silverdale bank.

Having just descended the bank from Silverdale, the 8-car DMU charter, 1T06 Birmingham New Street to Holditch Colliery, heads for Apedale Junction on a very rainy 22 October 1989. The lamp bracket of the first DMU car carries 'The Institution of Mining Engineers' plaque.

Making a good impression on the steep bank up to Silverdale on 22 April 1982, class 25s, 25208 and 25075 are about to pass Silverdale Ground Frame before entering the station and if cleared, onward to Madeley Chord.

During March 1987, the siding at Silverdale was extended in order to accommodate longer MGR trains. On 22 March 1987, class 47, 47362 is seen here at Silverdale Church with an engineer's train and a Plasser & Theurer GPC 12ton crane.

On 16 June 1987, vandal activity at Silverdale caused an Ironbridge Power Station MGR train to derail just south of the station and close the line for two days. In this view, an HAA is slewed across both tracks with the Crewe breakdown train in attendance.

This picture, taken on 18 August 1985, shows Silverdale station building still in use as a mess room and office for the train crews and shunters. Class 47, 47381 is just running round its train of Ironbridge MGRs in order to propel them through the coal loader.

An atmospheric scene at Silverdale on 22 April 1982, looking in the direction of Keele tunnel, as a coal train from Holditch passes through with 25208 and 25075 providing the motive power. On the other line, 47197 propels a rake of MGRs through the loader whilst the opposite platform still has its passenger waiting shelter. The shelter however did not remain there much longer as it was recovered from Silverdale by railway preservationists based at Cheddleton and rebuilt there as a feature on Cheddleton Stations' platform two.

On 3 September 1986, after loading the train at Silverdale, class 20s 20005 and 20177 pick their way over the points and head into Keele Tunnel with an Ironbridge Power Station MGR working. The locomotives are going to work hard from this point as the line climbs through the 400yrd tunnel and all the way up to Keele station. (Peter Rawlins)

In this view, the climb from Silverdale is apparent as 20141 and 20121 emerge from Keele Tunnel with an MGR train bound for Ironbridge Power Station on 19 March 1987.

Just starting on the 1 in 200 down grade towards Madeley Chord, class 31 (unusual for this line) 31414 passes the site of Keele Station with an engineers train on 18 May 1988.

On a sunny Sunday afternoon in July 1981, Keele Station is submiting to nature having closed 7 May 1956. The structure appeared to be in vandal-free condition, probably because of its remote location. The station was eventually demolished in 1986.

The single platform remains at Keele Station on 20 March 1987, as class 20s, 20140 and 20051 pass the site with Ironbridge Power Station MGR 'empties' towards Silverdale.

At the Madeley Chord end of the Silverdale branch, 20121 and 20141 are seen here running round a train of Ironbridge Power Station MGRs having just arrived from Silverdale. The locomotives will then couple to the far end of the train and proceed down the chord (left of picture) to join the West Coast Mainline. One of the platforms of the former Madeley Road Station is still in place when this picture was taken on 18 March 1987. Two years later a new 'station' building was erected on this platform as an engineers' facility.

Just beyond Madeley Road Station, in the direction of Market Drayton, the line seen curving away to the right, continues as single track for approximately ¼ mile. In this picture taken on 18 March 1987, 20141 and 20121 have just uncoupled from their train to run round having arrived from Silverdale. The whole area is now completely over grown.

6. HOLDITCH COLLIERY RAILWAY

Holditch Colliery in Chesterton is an ancient industrial site; archaeological investigations revealed that coal had been worked in the area for more than 2000 years. The colliery, known locally as Brymbo, came into operation in 1912. It got its name from the original owners, the Brymbo Steel Works based in Wrexham, which in the early years used almost the entire output of coal for their own steel plant. Managed later on by the Shelton Iron, Steel & Coal Company, Holditch was also a very gas rich colliery and supplied large amounts of gas to local brickworks. It was the last pit in the area to use steam-powered machinery, and steam locomotives were still in use after all the other collieries had abandoned them. Remarkably, its steam driven winding engines were not phased out until 1980. These pictures show the remaining colliery locomotives at work in 1983, none of which were new to Holditch, they all came second hand from other pits in the area. Holditch Colliery closed in 1989 and the site is now occupied by a major industrial estate.

On 3 February 1983, Bagnall 220HP 0-6-0 locomotive 'Hem Heath No 3D' waits while the shunter uncouples two internal-use mineral wagons to act as barrier wagons. This is the commencement of the BR section as it enters the colliery and although there is a run-off area into an embankment, seen just behind the wagons, these wagons were placed there as 'belt & braces'.

At the controls of 'Hem Heath No 3D', on 3 February 1983, is long serving driver/fitter Mr R.G Burnett. Mr Burnett, who was about to retire at the end of March that year, started at Holditch in 1945 working mostly on steam engines, recollecting two 0-4-0 saddle tanks in particular – 'Cornish' and 'Dilhorne'.

'Hem Heath No 3D' was built by Bagnalls at their Stafford works in 1956, delivered straight to Hem Heath Colliery. On 1 February 1968, it transferred to Silverdale Colliery where it worked until 10 July 1971 when the loco then moved to Holditch. In this photograph taken on 3 February 1983, a sign of things to come is seen in the distance as a new road-vehicle coal loader is brought into use.

Looking at this scene at Holditch in 1983, with its brand new coal washing and grading plant, it did not seem possible that in the space of 6 years the colliery would be closed down. Everything in this view has now disappeared and it is difficult to imagine that a colliery ever existed here.

A sad site at Holditch on 3 February 1983, as this 0-6-0 locomotive lies derelict in the colliery yard. Built by Bagnalls in 1958 as works number 3134, 'Hem Heath 4D' came to Holditch from that colliery in the late 1960s but was out of use by 1970. The loco was finally scrapped on site in 1984

Inside the loco shed at Holditch on 3 February 1983 resides freshly painted Vanguard diesel hydraulic 0-6-0 'No 13D'. This loco, built by Thomas Hill in 1967, came to Holditch from Chatterley Whitfield Colliery in 1976. However, in 1989 it returned to Chatterley Whitfield Mining Museum as an exhibit.

A view of the new loco shed built at Holditch, with 'Hem Heath No 3D' at the fuelling point. Fitted out as a full maintenance facility, it was complete with inspection pits, oil store and diesel fuel bunkering.

7. SHELTON BAR RAILWAY

Shelton Bar was a 400-acre steelworks in the city of Stoke-on-Trent and at its peak; the works employed more than 10,000 people. It had five coalmines, a complete railway system and a by-products factory. The main site began in 1830 and was rapidly developed in the 1840s by the fourth Earl Granville. Various coal mines were also sunk around the site and miles of railway constructed. By 1920, it had become a very efficient steelworks. During World War 2, it was a frequent target for German bombers, since it was almost impossible to fully blackout the light from the enormous blast furnaces. Shelton Bar was eventually nationalised after the war and the main smelting works closed in 1978. The eastern side of the complex, around 200 acres, was reclaimed for the 1986 Stoke-on-Trent National Garden Festival. When the roll-ing mill opened in 1964 it was the world's first continuous cast production mill, and it remained operational, without interruption, even during the Garden festival operations. However, the entire works was closed by British Steel in 1999 but in 2002 the area and internal railway was in use again as a major rail and ballast supply depot for the £8 billion upgrade of the West Coast Main Line railway, which runs past the site. During the early months of 2005 the half-mile long rolling mill sheds were finally demolished and the site is now being transformed as part of a major £120 million regeneration project. These pictures show a working railway when the rolling mill was at its busiest in the 1980s, as steel billets or 'blooms' were brought into the mill from Scunthorpe and went out as finished products.

Yorkshire Engine Company 0-6-0 diesel-electric 'JANUS' stands for the camera with driver Peter Claveley and shunter John Furnival and its train of finished steel beams, on 12 February 1986. The train, seen here alongside the half-mile long rolling mill sheds, was about to be taken down to the exchange sidings at Etruria.

In this view, 'JANUS' is about to be uncoupled to run around its train before its a long decent down the branch to Etruria Sidings, while Transport Manager John Carr, wearing the white hat, checks the condition of a rail joint. 12 February 1986.

Shelton Bar had a very extensive railway system, which can be appreciated in this view as 'JANUS', photographed on12 February 1986, arrives at the top of the steep climb from the exchange sidings at Etruria. The line to the extreme left formed part of the old NSRs Grange Branch, and now used as sidings. Built by the Yorkshire Engine Co in 1962, as works number 2772, 'JANUS' worked on site until closure in 1999.

Amid the deafening noise from the rolling mill, Yorkshire 0-6-0 'ATLAS' emerges from the main shed on 12 February 1986 with a train of 'Shelton' products. 'ATLAS' was built in 1961 as works number 2787 and came straight to Shelton Bar. It also remained in service until closure but its fate is unknown.

Another Yorkshire Engine Co product was 200HP 0-4-0 diesel electric locomotive 'WEASEL'. Built in 1960 as works number 2783, it was out of use by 1989 and scrapped on site in 1996. It is seen here on 12 February 1986 outside the shed used for locomotive maintenance.

The other 0-4-0 loco in use at Shelton Bar in the 1980s was 'BADGER' also built by the Yorkshire Engine Co. and seen here outside the maintenance building with a single bogie flat. 'BADGER' was built in 1962, works number 2869 and worked throughout its life at Shelton but unfortunately scrapped in 1996. Both of the 0-4-0 locomotives operated mainly at the works level as they lacked the power to work trains out of Etruria Sidings. 12 February 1986.

Inside the loco shed on 12 February 1986, undergoing heavy maintenance, is the other 600HP 0-6-0 locomotive 'LUDSTONE'. Another Yorkshire engine built in 1962 as works number 2868, this loco worked through out its life at Shelton until the works closed in 1999. Fortunately, this engine survived and it now resides at the Foxfield Railway, Blythe Bridge.

8. WOLSTANTON COLLIERY RAILWAY

The first records of a Wolstanton mine indicate that in 1916 it provided ironstone only for the local ironworks. The colliery commenced operations a few years later when a group of Pottery companies invested in the company for it to establish a coalmine at the site, which then became known as Wolstanton Colliery. The pit continued under this management until its nationalisation in 1947. Major reconstruction started in 1950 and when this was completed 14 years later a preparation plant, railway sidings and washing facilities had been constructed.

By the time these pictures were taken in 1983, very little change had taken place. During 1975, Wolstanton made an underground connection with Chatterley Whitfield Colliery and it was then able to claim to be the Super pit of North Staffordshire, having the deepest shaft in Western Europe – measuring 3759 feet. The Colliery closed entirely in 1985 with a huge loss of jobs and by 1986, in almost uncivil haste, the land was cleared and the shafts capped. An ASDA superstore and out-of-town retail park now occupy the site.

With Senior Driver Mr J Barnish at the controls, Bagnall 0-6-0 diesel electric 'Wolstanton No 1' brings a rake of internal-use wagons past the camera on 3 February 1983. The loco was new to Wolstanton being built in 1959 as works number 3147. It worked there until the colliery closed and it was sold as scrap to Booths of Rotherham in 1986. To the right of the picture are the massive rolling mill sheds of Shelton Bar Steel Works, which was the other side of the main Stoke-Manchester main line.

on 3 February 1983, at the Land Sale Wharf end of the sidings at Wolstanton, Bagnall 0-6-0 'Wolstanton no 3' brings a rake of NCB mineral wagons to be offloaded at the wharf. 'Wolstanton No3' was built in 1960, allocated works number 3150, and started its life at Hem Heath Colliery working there until 1962 when it transferred to Wolstanton. When the pit closed in 1985, it was rescued by the Foxfield Railway and is now at Blythe Bridge.

Taken from the cab of 'No3', looking back over the train towards the coal preparation plant and loading area, this view gives an indication of the vast size of this part of the coal disposal area at Wolstanton. The colliery is actually some distance away on the other side of the A500 'D road', to the left of the picture. Coal from the pit, was transported to the washers on enclosed elevated conveyors across the A500 road. A similar conveyor system also transported coal over the main railway line at Etruria directly to Shelton Bar and this is visible at the extreme right of the picture.

This is a picture of the two-road loco shed at Wolstanton, situated south of the coal preparation plant towards the Etruria end of the extensive wagon storage sidings. Seen here outside the shed on 3 February 1983, is Ruston diesel hydraulic 0-6-0 locomotive, 'Victoria No D2'. Built at the Ruston works in 1965 (works number 512845) it was delivered new to the Victoria Colliery, Biddulph, Stoke-on-Trent. The locomotive relocated to Wolstanton in 1976 and retained its original name throughout its stay, being sold to Booths of Rotherham in 1986.

Inside the locomotive shed is another 204HP Bagnall 0-6-0, 'Wolstanton No 1'. This loco, built in 1959 as works number 3147, was new to Wolstanton Colliery. It worked throughout its time at the colliery and eventually went to Booths of Rotherham for scrapping in 1986. Picture taken 3 February 1983.

Seen here in the exchange sidings is a Thomas Hill Vanguard-type 0-6-0 Diesel locomotive 'No 12D'. It was delivered new to Chatterley Whitfield Colliery in 1967 and transferred to Wolstanton in 1976, where it remained in service until 1985 when it was sold to Booths of Rotherham for scrap. An MGR has just arrived in the sidings and is waiting for 'No 12D's attention. Behind the MGR, the overhead lines of the Stoke-Manchester main line are just visible. The sidings here were quite extensive and located on two levels. In total, the internal railway at Wolstanton extended to over ten miles. 3 February 1983.

Taken on 3 February 1983, this picture shows 'Wolstanton No 5' standing outside the washing plant and out of use. This Bagnall 0-6-0, builders number 3123, was delivered new to Littleton Colliery, Cannock in 1957. Twenty years later, it came to Wolstanton, working intermittently until it was condemned and scrapped on site before the pit closed in 1985.

9. CHATTERLEY WHITFIELD MUSEUM RAILWAY

Chatterley Whitfield Colliery, situated between Chell Heath and Ball Green, Stoke-on-Trent, is reputed to be one of the most intact preserved collieries in the United Kingdom that illustrates the development of a Victorian colliery. The mine sunk in 1838 expanded throughout the decades to become the first mine in Britain to produce a million tons of coal in one year. At its peak, 4,000 people worked at the pit. However, following a general decline in coal demand in the 1970s the mine closed in 1977. Following closure, it developed into a mining museum. It was the first of its kind, with visitors making an actual cage decent underground. However, this particular part of the mine shared its water drainage with pumps from nearby Wolstanton Colliery. When Wolstanton closed in 1986, the underground section at Whitfield also shut down. In October 1987, Princess Anne opened a 'mock' underground feature, which unfortunately was not successful. Whilst all this was happening a group of enthusiasts and mining museum staff became involved, during the late 80s, in reinstating part of the once extensive railway network at the site. The following pictures illustrate the progress made at the time, which showed tremendous promise until it all ended in 1993. With no further financial support from the museum forthcoming, it closed down along with the colliery site, the locomotives, and other railway artefacts auctioned off that same year. This was an opportunity for railway preservation in North Staffordshire, sadly overlooked.

The date on the side of the wagon gives a clue to when this picture might have been taken. It was in fact 29 April 1990 and 0-4-OST Robert Heath No 6 steams towards Whitfield Road crossing on a demonstration. In the background, the magnificent headgear of the Hesketh Pit dwarfs its surroundings. The large building on the right of the picture houses the huge Hesketh Steam Winding Engine.

This picture is a view of Chatterley Whitfield Colliery in March 1982. Although the last coal was drawn in 1977, some of the workshops and laboratory remained open. The cars seen here at the old railway crossing are taking a short cut through the colliery from Biddulph Road to Ball Green. This access road is now closed and is only available to commercial occupiers of the site.

This atmospheric view, taken in March 1982, looks in the direction of Ball Green. The plume of steam emerging near the Hesketh Winding House indicates that the colliery's steam boilers were still being charged to provide energy and heating. At this time, the 'real' underground experience could be enjoyed as visitors made a 700-foot cage ride into the Winstanley Pit.

By 1987, the 'underground' experience at Whitfield could only be taken in the new enclosed surface building, which artificially recreated mining conditions for visitors. When this picture was taken on 11 January 1987, local railway enthusiasts and museum staff had started to lay track for a standard gauge railway feature. The concrete structure on the left housed the new 'underground' experience.

On 11 January 1987, this view shows the track alignment for the new railway at Whitfield. Behind the camera is a head shunt running for approximately 150 metres. The right hand line ran past the Hesketh building and into the loco shed and yard. The line to the left ran for about a quarter mile, crossing the internal road under the coal screens, following an original alignment down to the former wagon sidings.

Transferred from Holditch Colliery, Bagnall 0-6-0 'Hem Heath No 3' is seen at Chatterley Whitfield Mining Museum, in the company of the other ex-Holditch 0-6-0 engine, Vanguard 'No 13D', on 1 September 1987.

The museum was still acquiring rolling stock for preservation in the 1990s and seen here on 17 March 1991, an Ex-LMS 20T brake van had recently arrived from Hem Heath Colliery.

One of the museum's railway demonstration days took place on 29 April 1990 and in this picture, taken by the engine shed, 'Robert Heath No 6' 0-4-0ST is in steam alongside Yorkshire Engine Co 1952-built 0-6-0ST 'No 9' which at this time required substantial restoration.

The single road engine shed at Whitfield, seen here on 1 September 1987, had a fully equipped workshop. On the left is Manning Wardle 0-6-0ST 'Welshman' and in the centre is a Yorkshire Engine Co 400HP 0-6-0 diesel electric locomotive. This engine, built in 1960 (works number 2745) came from Agecroft Colliery, Manchester. It was sold to the South Devon Railway, Buckfastleigh in 1994.

Volunteers and museum staff at Whitfield carried out a lot of restoration work on locomotives and rolling stock. In this picture, taken on 23 October 1988, 'Hem Heath No 3' diesel loco had been repaired and repainted and is seen coupled to a restored BR 20T brake van.

This picture shows Robert Heath No 6, on a demonstration run at Whitfield on 5 April 1992. The 0-4-0 saddle tank was built in 1885 by Robert Heath for use at the company's Black Bull colliery. Rebuilt in 1934 it worked under the auspices of the National Coal Board until it donated the locomotive to Staffordshire County Council's Museum at Shugborough Hall in 1969 to become part of a collection of railway artefacts. 'No 6' stayed at Shugborough until the early 1980s when the exhibits were dispersed, and No 6 moved to the Chatterley Whitfield Mining Museum on 16 November 1983. The locomotive, then in remarkably good condition, was rebuilt to working order by Dorothea Restoration Projects and loaned to the National Garden Festival site at Etruria, from May to October 1986. When the mining museum closed in 1993 a group of members from the Foxfield Railway were determined that 'No 6' should not leave the area and at the auction held at Chatterley Whitfield in April 1994 it was purchased, and moved to Foxfield. It remains there today in full working order.

'Robert Heath No 6' again having just crossed the Whitfield Road, storms up the bank towards the head shunt over an original alignment of the colliery's former sidings.

This picture could easily be mistaken for one taken in the 1960s. In fact it was 5 April 1992 and 0-6-0ST 'Joseph' heads under the screens at Chatterley Whitfield Mining Museum during a demonstration run. 'Joseph' is one of two Hudswell Clarke locos built in 1943. 'Joseph' and the other locomotive, 'Robert' both worked at Bold Colliery until the early 1980s. In 1988 they were transferred to Whitfield and by early January 1989 both locomotives were taken to the Crewe Heritage Centre for restoration. Only 'Joseph' was restored to full working order and 'Robert' remains dismantled at The Railway Age, Crewe.

BIBLIOGRAPHY

Whilst compiling North Staffordshire Railways Scenes from the 1980s I referred to various sources, including the following publications, some of which are now out of print.

Baker, Allan C. *The Potteries Loop Line* (Trent Valley Publications)

Baker, Allan C. *Stoke and North Staffordshire Railways* (Irwell Press)

Baker, Allan C. *The Iron, Steel and Coal Industry of North Staffordshire* (Irwell Press)

Clark, P.L. *Staffordshire Railways* (Staffordshire County Library)

Jeuda, Basil *The Leek, Caldon and Waterhouses Railway* (North Staffordshire Railway Company 1978 Ltd)

Lester, C.R. *The Stoke to Market Drayton Line* (The Oakwood Press)

Marsden, Colin J. *Departmental Stock* (Ian Allan)

Marsden, Colin J. *BR and Private Owner Wagons* (Ian Allan)

Oppitz, Leslie *Lost Railways of Staffordshire* (Countryside Books)

Waterhouse, Richard *North Staffordshire Steam Railway Centre Guide* (1st Edition) (North Staffordshire Railway Company 1978 Ltd)

INDEX